An opini

BRIGHTON

Written by
JOE MINIHANE

Photography by
ELLEN RICHARDSON

Hove Beach (no.44)

4

BONSAI PLANT KITCHEN

Unrivalled plant-based Asian cuisine

Starting as a delivery pop-up during lockdown, Bonsai Plant Kitchen opened in its current location in 2022. Since then, it has become a word-of-mouth smash. Co-founder Arlo has combined their passion for plant-based food with business partner Dom's hard-won ability to create next-level dishes from across Asia. Having returned to Vietnam seven times to train with local chefs, Dom worked with Arlo to create a menu that is entirely vegan but designed to satisfy everyone. The results are phenomenal. The tempura 'sea bream' made using pea protein and nori is succulent and beautiful, while the yakitori skewers are a triumph. The house kimchi and dirty rice are other stand-outs. Go immediately.

44–45 Baker Street, BN1 4JN
bonsaiplantkitchen.co.uk

3

THE LITTLE
FISH MARKET

Impeccable food from one of Brighton's finest chefs

The Little Fish Market is a small restaurant with a huge reputation. Regularly topping polls as the best place to eat in Brighton and Hove, the attention to detail in both the cooking and the dining room is sensational. Chef and owner Duncan Ray is a true visionary, creating a tasting menu that changes throughout the week depending on the ingredients he's able to source, which are always of the highest quality. The TLFM Egg & Soldiers is the only dish you're guaranteed to get whenever you come – a hollowed-out eggshell layered with puréed Jerusalem artichoke, smoked haddock jelly, acidulated cream and passion fruit. It's unlike anything you'll have eaten before.

10 Upper Market Street, BN3 1AS
thelittlefishmarket.co.uk

2

PLATEAU

Natural wines and small plates

Plateau's drinks list makes it the best spot in Brighton for those swept up by the increasingly popular natural wine movement, with bottles from some of Europe's hottest vineyards served in a welcoming, smartly designed space. There's a full-bodied Cabernet Franc from the Loire Valley, perfect for a winter evening spent hunkered down in the warm embrace of the main dining room, while the orange-hued skin contact white from Austria is best sipped on the street side seats at the height of summer. Sustenance comes in the form of a changing menu of small plates sourced from local producers, whether that's from fishermen landing their haul from south coast day boats or farmers rearing lamb in the South Downs.

1 Bartholomews, BN1 1HB
plateaubrighton.co.uk

1

THE CHILLI PICKLE

An Indian street food-infused institution

The Chilli Pickle is unquestionably the best place for South Asian food in Brighton, with dishes taking their inspiration from across the subcontinent. Lunch is all about the Grand Thalis, served with dhal, rice, pickles, chutney and chapati. Go for the corn and spinach pakora kadhi or the Goan fish curry made with locally caught sea bass. The dinner menu leans heavily on sharing, but there are plenty of solo dishes too. Start with gol gappa (crispy shells stuffed with a potato and onion masala) and follow it up with the Kashmiri lamb cutlets, Punjabi aubergine curry and masala fries. Vegans and veggies are properly looked after, with the chole masala chickpea curry a highlight.

17 Jubilee Street, BN1 1GE
thechillipickle.com

Saturday evening

Head for dinner at Bincho Yakitori (no.6) before drinks at Hand in Hand (no.54) or The Well (no.52). Hit the dance-floor at Legends (no.57) for the ultimate Brighton clubbing experience.

Sunday brunch

Shake off the evening's excesses with brunch at Fika (no.18) before a stroll around Preston Park (no.39). Stock up on the best new tunes at Resident (no.22), get your fill of designer fashion at Our Daily Edit (no.27) and Peggs & Son (no.34), then peruse the shelves at City Books (no.35).

Sunday afternoon

After hitting the arcades on the Palace Pier (no.42), pop into The Geese (no.9) for a roast, before a wander through the opulent halls of the Royal Pavilion (no.48) and the fascinating Brighton Museum and Art Gallery (no.46).

Sunday evening

Have a pint at The Great Eastern (no.55), then watch the latest art-house flick at the Duke of York's cinema (no.47). Finish the weekend with Brighton's best vegan food at Bonsai Plant Kitchen (no.4).

A PERFECT WEEKEND

Friday night

Check in at Lansdowne House (no.50) and head around the
corner for dinner at The Little Fish Market (no.3). Grab a late-
night pint or two at The Bee's Mouth (no.53), then get a good
night's rest before a big weekend.

Saturday morning

Ease off the previous evening with a swim at Sea Lanes (no.37),
followed by a sauna at the nearby Beach Box Spa (no.43). Settle
down to breakfast at Egg & Spoon (no.16) before exploring
Sussex Square and Kemptown's majestic Georgian architecture
(no.40).

Saturday lunch

Make a coffee stop at Loam (no.19) before wandering around
North Laine, stopping off to pick up bric-a-brac at Snoopers
Paradise (no.23) and the best vintage at Wolf & Gypsy (no.29).
Feast on a delicious thali at The Chilli Pickle (no.1) or have a
leisurely lunch at Burnt Orange (no.11).

Saturday afternoon

Hire bikes and cycle along the awe-inspiring Undercliff Path
to Saltdean (no.38), then get a caffeine fix and post-workout
sweet treat at Dharma Coffee (no.20).

BRIGHTON MOD WEEKENDER

Started by New Untouchables, a group dedicated to modernist and 1960s underground culture, the Brighton Mod Weekender harks back to the days of pitch battles between mods and rockers by the pier. These days things are more sedate, with cover bands, a chance to admire classic fashion and, of course, the vintage scooters that fill Madeira Drive from dawn until dusk.

August / newuntouchables.com

VETERAN CAR RUN

Tracing its history to an 1896 Act of Parliament that raised the speed limit to 14 mph, the first Veteran Car Run from London to Brighton took place in 1899. Today, it attracts hundreds of vintage cars, all of which must have been built before 1905. The majestic sight of these classic vehicles making their merry way to the seafront is one of the highlights of the autumn.

November / veterancarrun.com

BURNING THE CLOCKS

Celebrating the winter solstice since 1987, Burning the Clocks sees locals parade through the city with paper and willow lanterns on 21 December. These creations are then placed on a huge bonfire on the beach to mark the turning of the year and the promise of lighter days to come.

December / samesky.co.uk

SEASONAL EVENTS

BRIGHTON MARATHON

Ten thousand runners set off from Preston Park on a route that passes the Royal Pavilion, heads out along the cliff tops towards Rottingdean, then swings back all the way towards Hove, finishing on the Lawns. The spring air and buzzing crowds make this one of the city's biggest annual events.

April / brightonmarathonweekend.co.uk

LONDON TO BRIGHTON BIKE RIDE

The London to Brighton bike ride became official in 1976, but the history of cycling from the capital to the coast goes all the way back to 1869, when three pioneers undertook the route. Today, thousands of riders head from Clapham Common out of London and through the Downs, tackling the brutal climb over Ditchling Beacon before freewheeling down to the seafront, all in the name of charity.

June / bhf.org.uk

BRIGHTON PRIDE

The most popular Pride event in the UK, Brighton's annual celebration of its vital LGBTQ+ community sees around 300,000 people descend on the city. While the party village in Kemptown and festival site in Preston Park pull in partygoers, it's the parade from Hove that's the main event, keeping at its heart the importance of ensuring that everyone is welcome.

August / brighton-pride.org

deceptively wonderful boardwalk and the incredible Sea Lanes (no.37), home to a 50-metre heated pool, coffee spot and bar, where the action is friendly, sometimes lively, but never lairy.

Of course, Brighton is about so much more than the beach. Its shopping is rightly lauded, thanks to a preponderance of excellent vintage stores in the North Laine area and a thriving set of independent book and record shops. Throw in a seemingly never-ending number of top-rated coffee stops and a restaurant scene bursting with creativity, and there's a chance to see an easier side of seaside life without the hectic atmosphere.

That's not to decry the city's amazing nightlife. Cosy pubs come into their own in winter, supplying the best local beers and spirits with a soundtrack provided by DJs who prove that Brighton has the finest music nerds in the nation. The amazing LGBTQ+ scene offers year-round entertainment that is fun, safe and a joy for all. And indie venues serve up the best new bands, with sticky floors and a welcoming vibe to match.

Come to Brighton at any time of year and you'll have a blast. This is a city that thrums with life and is all the better when you avoid the usual tourist traps for something vibrant and authentic. All the hand-picked spots in this book are just that.

Joe Minihane, Brighton, 2023

WHAT MAKES
BRIGHTON BRILLIANT?

Ever since Lewes-born Dr Richard Russell espoused the therapeutic benefits of Brighton's seawater in 1750, the place that was once the tiny fishing village of Brighthelmstone has been pulling in tourists keen for bracing air and a bit of a knees-up. Once the Prince Regent set up camp here in the late 18th century, overseeing the construction of his iconic Pavilion (no.48), Brighton's place as England's ultimate seaside getaway was assured.

Trains from London began running in 1841, ushering in a boom that continues to this day. The chance to pull up a deckchair as the waves rolled in proved the ideal tonic for the capital's worn-out working classes. And yet, arrive by rail today and it can be easy to fall into the trap that thousands of others do, the glint of the English Channel as you emerge from the station proving too tempting to explore the alternatives. Before you know it, you're paying upwards of £7 for a pint in a second-rate seafront pub while being serenaded with a karaoke version of 'Wonderwall'. Throw in hordes of hen and stag parties, and the stretch of beach between the ruins of the West Pier and the jollity of the Palace Pier (no.42) can feel a bit too booze-soaked.

Avoiding the chaos, however, is mercifully easy. If you want to kick back on the beach, Hove's lawn-backed sweep is a huge favourite with locals and young families. Meanwhile Kemptown's pebbles have been rejuvenated thanks to a

Ditchling Beacon (no.41)
Opposite: North Laine

Harbour Hotel (no.49)

Stoney Point owner Jesse (no.17)
Opposite: Plateau (no.2)

INFORMATION IS DEAD. LONG LIVE OPINION.

You can find everything you need to know about Brighton online.

Except you won't find a selection of highly curated, personal recommendations like this. This is an unashamedly opinionated series, and we'll only tell you about the places that we really like. But we're a small, indie publisher in Hackney – why should you listen to us? Because although we're not based in Brighton, we've spent plenty of time wandering the Lanes, eating at the many delicious seasonal restaurants the city has to offer and wincing our way across the pebbles to the sea. We love Brighton, and here are the places that make it so great.

Other opinionated guides:

East London

London Architecture

Vegan London

London Green Spaces

Independent London

London Pubs

Sweet London

Kids' London

Escape London

Eco London

Big Kids' London

Art London

Free London

Queer London

London Delis

London Hotels

Historic London

Margate

6

BINCHO YAKITORI

A taste of Japan close to the seafront

Creating a proper izakaya outside of Japan can't be done without deep knowledge and respect of the late-night hang-outs found in the country's biggest cities. But David Miney has achieved it with Bincho Yakitori. Working as a chef in Tokyo, he became obsessed with izakayas and brought home a crack team of Japanese chefs to set up this incredible place. You'll need to book well in advance, but it'll be worth the wait. The yakitori (skewers of perfectly fried meat) are sublime. While the menu changes every week, everything they serve is sure to be exquisite, from pork belly to mouth-watering shiitake mushrooms. A sake menu offers tipples from across Japan, while the beer selection is outrageously good. Try the Monsuta, a crisp and delicious lager from Okinawa.

63 Preston Street, BN1 2HE
binchoyakitori.com

7

CIN CIN

Hove's standout Italian serving amazing pasta

Brighton has old-school Italian restaurants galore, but none can match the killer bowls of pasta on offer at Cin Cin. At the heart of the dining room is the open kitchen, with a surrounding bar where hungry guests can chat with the chefs as they pull together dishes using the freshest pasta this side of Turin. The menu changes month by month, but look out for the likes of caramelle – pasta parcels that come filled with pea, mint and potato – or paccheri with squid, courgettes and preserved lemon. There are vegetarian, vegan and gluten-free menus, plus a wine list that stars favourites from across Italy.

60 Western Road, BN3 1JD
cincin.co.uk

8

THE POND

North Laine boozer serving incredible bao buns

Its own delicious Pondwater Pale Ale makes The Pond a handy stop-off for a pint whenever North Laine's busy streets get too much. But it's the Taiwanese buns from resident pop-up Baby Bao that make this pub special. The menu changes slightly with the seasons, but classic options include panko squash or pork belly with spring onions and peanuts. The buns are light, fluffy and as good as anything you'll find in Taipei. Make sure you leave room for the spicy Korean wings and the impossible-to-resist house fries, which come coated in hoisin sauce. These aren't for sharing; you'll inhale the entire bowl within seconds. There are plenty of vegan and veggie options, the jackfruit karaage a particular stand-out.

49 Gloucester Road, BN1 4AQ
thepondbrighton.com

9

THE GEESE

The local with the best roasts

The Geese is a first-class community pub, with regulars crowding the bar and spreading out at tables positioned alongside the vast street-side windows. It also serves the best Sunday roast in the city, where portions are generous, roast potatoes are cooked to perfection and veggies and vegans don't have to put up with a bone-dry nut roast (beetroot and sweet potato Wellington or veggie sausage options make for a proper alternative). The Wednesday night two-for-£20 sausage and mash deal is legendary: try the gluten-free venison and apple sausages paired with bone marrow mash and prepare to be dozing over your pint come last orders.

16 Southover Street, BN2 9UA
thegeesebrighton.com

10

WILD FLOR

Hove restaurant with a focus on local produce

What makes Wild Flor special is that it's so clearly rooted in the Sussex food scene. The first thing you'll notice stepping into this small stripped-back restaurant is a blackboard displaying the provenance of all its produce. Meat comes from Saddlescombe Farm, north of the city, while fruit and veg are sourced via Brighton-based Shrub Provisions. Owners James and Faye Thomson have created a modern British menu built around seasonality. The real star is the set menu, available at lunchtime from Tuesday to Friday and dinner-time from Thursday to Saturday, where you can try three courses for £25 – incredible value for some of the finest cooking on the south coast.

42 Church Road, BN3 2FN
wildflor.com

11

BURNT ORANGE

All-day restaurant with first-rate sharing plates

Small plates rule the day at Burnt Orange, a lively and inviting hang-out that is heaving all year round. The food here is bold and the menu chock-full of true one-offs, notably the smoked lamb shoulder cigars – deep-fried meat-filled rolls paired with a yoghurt dip. The smoked miso aubergine is not to be missed either. The Experience menus, including options for carnivores and veggies, see the kitchen team pick the dishes, meaning all you need to do is peruse the excellent cocktail list. The Burnt Orange Martini is the loosener of choice around these parts, great for easing your way into a languid evening around the table.

59 Middle Street, BN1 1AL
burnt-orange.co.uk

12

EMBERS

Wood-fired fare from Brighton's hot new opening

Embers is the brainchild of Dave Marrow and Isaac Bartlett-Copeland, two chefs who made their name in Brighton's fine dining scene. There's no fussiness here, though. Rather, the action is centred on a huge, medieval-style fire cage, which sits at the heart of the open kitchen. It uses carbon-neutral wood from a lumberyard in Hassocks, north of the city, adding a delicious smokiness to the food. Small plates are the main pull, with the beef short rib, charred broccoli with sweetcorn cream and honey butter chicken essential. Centrepiece dishes, including a ludicrously good dry-aged pork tomahawk, are ideal for big groups. The service here is superb, with a welcoming bunch working the tables and mixing delicious drinks.

42 Meeting House Lane, BN1 1HB
embersbrighton.co.uk

13

THE SALT ROOM

Fish leads the line

Found opposite the West Pier, beneath the Hilton Hotel, The Salt Room is the place to go for seafood on the seafront. The cooking is simple and all the better for it. The best approach is to go all out: if you're eating in a big group, order the seafood platter to start, featuring succulent king prawns, mussels, calamari and scallops. Follow it with beautifully baked market fish, which changes throughout the week depending on availability; keep an eye out for the brill, served with garlic crushed potatoes and a seasonal salad. The sea-view terrace gets full when the weather hots up, but there's ample space inside – ideal if you want a breather from the crowds.

106 Kings Road, BN1 2FU
saltroom-restaurant.co.uk

14

KINDLING

Locally focused fine dining

Kindling's open kitchen and minimal aesthetic help make it one of the most enjoyable places to eat in Brighton. The focus is on sustainability and local ingredients, whether that's mutton from Saddlescombe Farm on the South Downs or seasonal fruit and vegetables from Chef's Farms in Storrington, West Sussex. The menu changes daily, with affordable small plates served at lunchtime and a blow-out tasting menu in the evening that is available with vegan, vegetarian, pescatarian and dairy-free options. Keep an eye out for cured trout and the mutton and Longhorn beef stew. The wine list is pleasingly succinct, while the booze-free cocktails, especially the No-groni, are an ideal way to kick off the evening.

69 East Street, BN1 1HQ
kindlingrestaurant.com

15

ETCH.
BY STEVEN EDWARDS

Tasting menus to suit all appetites and budgets

With *Masterchef: The Professionals* winner Steven Edwards at the helm, etch. is an indulgent joint, one where you put yourself in the hands of the friendly team and wait to be wowed. The tasting menu is available in nine-, seven- or five-course variations, but the recent addition of a more affordable – but no less impressive – 'Introduction to etch.' option, featuring four dishes, means it's now a winner for lunch as well as a leisurely dinner. The seasonal menu changes weekly, although every diner gets the renowned Marmite bread with seaweed butter to start. This is creative cooking without any snobbery.

214–216 Church Road, BN3 2DJ
etchfood.co.uk

16

EGG & SPOON

The best brunch in Brighton

Egg & Spoon in Kemptown Village serves up the best brunch, whether you want a hefty full English or something more exotic. The smart move is to opt for the latter, with the chicken schnitzel brioche and chilli scrambled eggs among the highlights. Classics such as eggs Benedict and eggs Florentine are prepared to perfection, and the presentation is top class whatever you order. Tables can be almost impossible to come by on weekends unless you arrive early, which is where its ready-to-go salad boxes come in, including a Buddha Box with hummus, falafel, rice and broccoli. Ideal for a beach picnic, especially paired with a freshly made smoothie.

107–108 St George's Road, BN2 1EA
eggandspooncafe.com

17

STONEY POINT

Perfectly brewed coffee and home-baked treats

Stoney Point's light-flooded, ultra-relaxed indoor space closed for good in 2020, leaving more than a few local caffeine addicts bereft. But in moving to a street-side coffee hatch with outdoor seating, owner Jesse has created a fully fledged bakery with a die-hard fan base. As well as having a magic touch when it comes to brewing delicious oat cappuccinos, he's also created a mouth-watering custard-soaked bun, a sweet addition to any morning pick-me-up. His eclectic taste in tunes means customers are treated to vintage bluegrass, classic hip-hop and ambient electronica while ordering or sitting under the trees outside. It's enough to forgive him for shutting his doors and depriving Brighton of its finest chill-out space.

15 Montpelier Place, BN1 3BF
stoneypoint.co

18

FIKA

Swedish treats and amazing fried egg sandwiches

As its name suggests, Fika is Swedish at heart, with cinnamon buns the size of your head and weapons-grade coffee roasted in-house (a delicious Brazilian and Ugandan blend). But there's plenty here for those with an appetite for more local fare to kick-start their day. The fried egg sandwiches lead the line: the D Yolker has two eggs, cheddar and chives in a brioche bun and costs just a fiver. Meanwhile, the hash browns have developed a Brighton-wide reputation as the ultimate morning side dish. Perfectly crisp and lacking the greasiness of the average rival, they make an ideal companion to a late breakfast and cortado.

1 Norton Road, BN3 3BE
Other location: Sea Lanes, 300 Madeira Drive, BN2 1BX
fikasussex.co.uk

19

LOAM

Third-wave coffee and the greatest cinnamon buns

Brighton and Hove's hippest coffee shops seem to be engaged in a battle to serve up not just the perfect cup but also the best cinnamon buns. Loam takes top spot when it comes to these sweet treats, with a doughy delight that goes easy on the granulated sugar. Paired with a long black, it's the best way to start the day in North Laine. They take caffeine very seriously here, as attested by the rotating cast of roasts and the collection of books on third-wave coffee. Hand-thrown artisan ceramics are on sale too, made by Norwich-based pottery by.noo. Just a few feet from the shoulder-to-shoulder buzz of Kensington Gardens, this is a pleasingly chilled and sharply designed space.

111 Gloucester Road, BN1 4AF
instagram.com/loam.brighton

20
DHARMA COFFEE

Bright and airy coffee joint with friendly staff

Dharma's coffee might just be the best this side of London, but that's not the whole story about this airy corner spot where Brighton meets Hove. What truly sets it apart is the service, unquestionably the friendliest in the city. The staff here are kind-hearted and warm, making Dharma a community haven. It's a space where everyone from the local street sweeper to skint artists and sea swimmers are welcomed and cherished. The result is somewhere people come to linger, whether over a laptop or with new friends made over a cup of freshly brewed filter coffee. It's the apotheosis of how the city opens its arms to all.

20 Western Road, BN3 1AE
Other location: 82 North Road, BN1 1YD
dharmacoffee.co.uk

21

KEMPTOWN BOOKSHOP

A rejuvenated mecca for literary lovers

When local historical fiction author Cathy Hayward took ownership of this 50-year-old shop in May 2022, it went from being a pleasant enough space to a spectacular community hub. Since her arrival, Hayward has started weekly story-time sessions for kids, hired a dedicated children's and young-adult bookseller and created a monthly subscription service that delivers the latest new releases to those who just can't make up their mind when trawling the shelves. With regular events including author Q&As and creative writing classes in the new cafe upstairs, Kemptown Bookshop stands as an example of what all the best independent shops should be: the heartbeat of their local area.

91 St George's Road, BN2 1EE
kemptownbookshop.co.uk

22

RESIDENT

A leading light in the UK's music scene

Adopted Brightonian Nick Cave reckons Resident is 'the best f*cking record shop in the country', and it's hard to argue. Resident has helped to super-charge the record store renaissance in the UK, its shop the ultimate destination for picking up the freshest new vinyl cuts and reissues. The staff are exceptional, not only thanks to their ludicrously broad knowledge but also because they make this a welcoming place without a hint of the snobbery that can be encountered in some second-hand record shops. Its in-store gigs are the stuff of legend; buy an LP to be in with a chance of getting a ticket to see the best live bands do their thing among the racks.

27–28 Kensington Gardens, BN1 4AL
resident-music.com

23

SNOOPERS PARADISE

Eclectic, bizarre and brilliant bric-a-brac

Snoopers is nothing short of iconic. It bills itself as 'the vintage shop of your dreams', but that hardly does justice to this wonderful, rambling emporium. Pass through its famous pink doors and you're confronted with a wildly broad second-hand book selection, ranging from Dickens through to 21st-century nature writing. Turn right, and you're just as likely to find a First World War great coat as you are a fascinator made from pigeon feathers. Head across to the other side of the shop to pick up a Panama hat or a first pressing of a Beatles LP. Chintz lampshades, ghastly animal ornaments and classic comics are just some of the other treats on offer.

7–8 Kensington Gardens, BN1 4AL
snoopersparadise.co.uk

24

PAPERSMITHS

Stationery for the discerning note taker

Smartphones and tablets are soulless alternatives to pen and paper. And the wonderful, lovingly curated Papersmiths proves it. Every single item sold in this Sydney Street institution is a must-buy for those who love to write, draw and doodle. There are striking daily planners from The Completist; natty and colourful Kaweco fountain pens; and sets of gorgeous Blackwing pencils made for life-long artists. Yes, it's expensive, but what's on offer here isn't just for those scribbling out shopping lists (not that there's anything wrong with having a LEUCHTTURM1917 heavyweight notepad expressly for this purpose). This is old school stationery at its very best.

21 Sydney Street, BN1 4EN
papersmiths.co.uk

25
UTILITY

Proper kitchenware for discerning home lovers

Utility is Brighton's independent alternative to big name Scandinavian brands that peddle low-cost, throwaway homewares and hardware. Nothing on sale here will break the bank, but such is its obsession with sourcing hard-wearing items that all of it will last. Baking trays and loaf tins from USA Pan will satisfy even the most fastidious of cake makers, while classic white and blue enamel crockery will set off any vintage-led kitchen. There's also a pleasing line in old-school cleaning products, from soda crystals to Sunlight soap, plus a weirdly impressive array of jars, including classic designs from Weck and Le Parfait – something for the preservers in your life.

28a North Road, BN1 1YB
utilitygreatbritain.co.uk

26
CAPSULE RECORDS

Try out LPs via Spotify

The latest addition to Brighton and Hove's record shop scene, Capsule's mid-century-infused decor and chunky sound system encourage customers to linger. The shop not only does a fine line in jazz, electronica, hip-hop and ambient new releases, classics and reissues, but also serves up a killer flat white to savour in the courtyard while you ponder which LPs to add to your collection. Each record carries a QR code sticker that shoppers can scan to gain insight into the artist and sample tracks via a Spotify embed. The team here respect the fact that vinyl is a major investment, hence the chance to pull up a seat and try before you buy.

37 Western Road, BN3 1AF
capsulerecords.co.uk

27

OUR DAILY EDIT

Well-selected pieces from designers across the globe

As the name suggests, Our Daily Edit is a shop that makes a big deal of its well-curated range of menswear, women's fashion and accessories, including candles and cosmetics. This is very much a designer-led space, with selvedge denim from gender-neutral east London label I And Me and bold, block-coloured dresses from LF Markey, showing the effort the team here puts into sourcing clothes from labels beyond what's found on the high street. Whatever you buy will make you look and feel the part. Affordable accessories such as RoToTo socks from Koryo, Japan, or air freshener from Earl of East mean you don't have to leave empty-handed.

23 Ship Street, BN1 1AD
ourdailyedit.com

28
WORKSHOP

One-off designs and minimal homewares

Workshop's focus on simple and sustainable design is evident the moment you step into its minimal store a short walk from the Lanes. Beautiful Hasami Porcelain plates and bowls from Nagasaki Prefecture sit artfully next to textured clay mugs from AR Ceramics, made by Mexican-born, London-based potter Andrea Roman. Modern Danish benches and chairs from Frama, made from Baltic birch, feature the neat lines synonymous with Scandinavian design, along with the price tag to match. If budget-blowing furniture feels a little too much, there are plenty of more affordable options, including scents and candles from brands like Apothecary. The Space, Workshop's pop-up shop showcasing new designers, is just over the road.

15c Prince Albert Street, BN1 1HF
workshopliving.co.uk

29

WOLF & GYPSY VINTAGE

Vintage clothes without the usual trawl

The musty whiff and crowded rails that mark out most of Brighton's vintage shops are mercifully absent at Wolf & Gypsy. A bright, airy space, it offers a well-curated and modern take on preloved clothes. The focus is mostly on womenswear, with carefully selected dresses, jeans, shirts and boots that don't require shoppers to spend hours trawling the racks to find the piece they didn't realise they wanted. A small range of new items is also available, including highly covetable hemp mules and clogs and affordable Ichendorf glassware. A menswear space in the back offers a fine line in worn denim and workwear. This is an ultra-stylish shop that lacks the air of superiority of similar stores.

30 Sydney Street, BN1 4EP
wolfandgypsyvintage.co.uk

30

THE LANES

Historic quarter with a special charm

The narrow, labyrinthine Lanes were fully built up during the late 18th century and mark the area where the fishing village of Brighthelmstone once stood. Some sections date back over 500 years. The cramped spaces can feel overly hectic in summer, but that's no reason not to explore the vintage jewellery shops and street-side cafes that give the Lanes their charm. The newly minted Hanningtons Lane, named after a department store that once stood on the site, is home to a vast green wall, street art that goes beyond the usual Banksy tribute acts, plus boutiques that will leave you feeling the pinch but like you've done local business a favour.

Located between Ship Street,
North Street and East Street, BN1

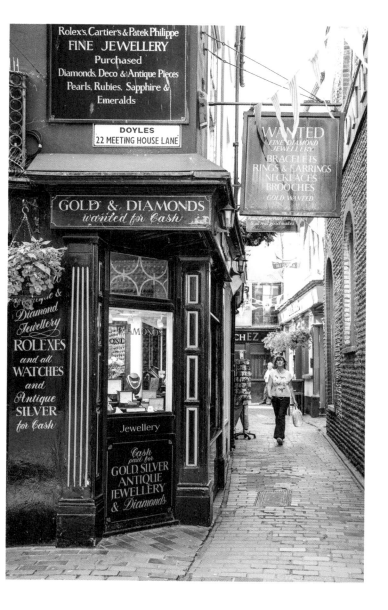

31

TIDY STREET GENERAL STORE

Well-sourced, high-end pieces

The name 'general store' might conjure images of an outpost on Main Street, Middle America. But this one on Tidy Street doesn't sell hardware or gardening tools. Rather, it's one of Brighton's coolest boutiques, specialising in understated pieces and carefully selected beauty products. Workwear jackets from French brand Vetra and Brighton-born Zoë Ward's handmade pinafore dresses and rain bags have pride of place alongside on-point jumpsuits from Japanese label Ichi Antiquités. Handwoven leather bags from Belgium-based Dragon Diffusion and skincare from Everyday Oil are just some of the other treats available. Definitely worth saving up for, the items on sale here will last forever.

102 Gloucester Road, BN1 4AP
tidystreetstore.com

32
HOLD

Hand-picked gifts that people actually want

HOLD bills itself as a 'lifestyle boutique', but that somewhat lofty assertion aside, this is a great gift shop. No Union Jack tat or sticks of rock here. Instead, HOLD is all about stuff that people actually want and will love, whether that's an MD Notebook all the way from Japan or a gender-neutral samphire scent from Laboratory Perfumes. Colourful and alluring soft furnishings from Stockholm-based Afroart, which highlights designs from small communities across Africa and Latin America, are another must-have. Wrap up your treats and send a message using Lagom Design paper and cards, made right here in Brighton.

14 Bond Street, BN1 1RD
hold.shop

33

ERA

Beautifully restored vintage furniture

There are ample opportunities to pick up old furniture in Brighton, especially in North Laine. And while a clapped-out mid-century desk chair might seem like a bargain, chances are it'll collapse within a month. Era, though, deals only in the very best quality. Owners Sam and Simon restore pieces to their original glory themselves and don't cut corners. Most of the stock dates from the 1940s and 50s, with hulking wartime Air Ministry desks sold alongside lovingly handmade and carefully refurbished G Plan tallboy drawers. You'll want to extend your credit limit before shopping, especially as they can arrange nationwide delivery. If you crave a home full of beautiful one-off pieces, this is the place to come.

92 Trafalgar Street, BN1 4ER
era-brighton.com

34

PEGGS & SON

Brighton's coolest menswear joint

Unquestionably the best menswear outlet in town, Peggs & Son is definitely not wallet-friendly. What's on offer, though, will last a lifetime. The collections here are pleasingly broad, from technical sportswear to Japanese jeans, way beyond the usual mod clobber found in other menswear spots across Brighton. The obsession with style and quality is apparent the second you step into this perfectly curated space. Turmeric-coloured sweatshirts from Danish brand Norse Projects sit neatly folded next to raw and selvedge denim from upstart English label Hawksmill. Snappy shirts from Folk are must-buy staples, as are Novesta's classic German Army Trainers. Regular sales mean there's always a chance to snap something up without paying top price.

39 Duke Street, BN1 1AG
peggsandson.com

35

CITY BOOKS

Friendly institution with knowledgeable staff

Run by booksellers Inge and Paul Sweetman in the Brunswick neighbourhood, the selection here is wide-ranging and carefully put together, with the latest hardbacks adorning the shelves by the counter and an excellent array of staff picks for those who want some guidance. Fiction is crammed into the rear of the store, with a low-ceilinged basement home to an impressive array of local history books and a music section to satisfy even the most hardcore fans. City Books also runs regular events in venues across the city, tying in with the biggest new releases. Past author Q&As include conversations with Ranulph Fiennes, Caitlin Moran and Elizabeth Day.

23 Western Road, BN3 1AF
city-books.co.uk

36

DOWSE

Sharp homewares and jewellery

The moment you walk into Dowse, its homewares, ceramics and jewellery feel like instant must-haves. Its idiosyncratic tube teapots and mugs are kitchen essentials for design obsessives, while the unique glass vases and plant pots make the ideal gifts for houseplant lovers. The jewellery is understated without ever feeling bland, with the team here having designed pieces for sale at London's Design Museum in the past. We also love the brash, stripy Bongusta towelling tote bags, made expressly for stashing wet beach kit after a day spent lounging on the pebbles.

37 Gardner Street, BN1 1UN
dowsedesign.co.uk

37

SEA LANES

Sparkling new beach-side pool

Sea Lanes is nothing short of sensational. Eight years in the making, this sharply designed development on Kemptown Beach houses a 50-metre outdoor pool, yoga studio and gym. Crucially, the pool is heated, making it a haven for swimmers when the sea temperature plummets or the wind whips in. It's also home to a branch of Fika (no.18), along with the Bison Beach Bar, which serves its own locally brewed beers, and Wood X Coal, a delicious barbecue joint. Its location, a 20-minute walk from the hectic stretch between the Palace and West Piers, means it has a more local vibe. This is an all-day destination, as good for breakfast as it is for a post-swim blow-out dinner with mates.

300 Madeira Drive, BN2 1BX
sealanesbrighton.co.uk

38

UNDERCLIFF PATH

An escape from the city

Running along the base of the chalk cliffs from the hideous Brighton Marina to the art deco-infused seaside village of Saltdean is the Undercliff Path. The flat three-mile route is great for a stroll, with vast sea views, but to get to Saltdean and back it's best to go on two wheels. Beryl BTN Bikes can be unlocked using a smartphone app and picked up along the seafront. These e-bikes make it easy on the thighs, but hiring a tandem from Brighton Beach Bikes, based by the Palace Pier, is a great way to share the load. Pack your swimming kit for a dip at Ovingdean Beach on the way and keep an eye out for seals flopping on the rocks.

Brighton Marina to Saltdean, BN2
brightonbeachbikes.co.uk
beryl.cc

39

PRESTON PARK

A shady retreat from the seafront

Brighton's largest green space, Preston Park is the best alternative to the beach for a summer picnic or an autumn stroll, especially when the broadleaf woodland begins to burnish in October. The main-line train to London clatters past its western flank, where colourful Victorian villas look out across the grassy expanse. The 19th-century velodrome, which surrounds the park's cricket pitch, hosts races throughout the summer. You can even clock up a few laps if you've brought your own wheels. Preston Manor, an 18th-century manor house rebuilt in the Edwardian period, claims to be one of Britain's most haunted buildings. A floating hand climbing a four-poster bed is unquestionably the most bizarre sighting, very much in keeping with Brighton's weirder side.

Preston Road, BN1 6SD

40

SUSSEX SQUARE

Explore Brighton's past through its buildings

Conceived in the early 1800s by property developer Thomas Kemp, the Kemptown estate remains Brighton's most striking example of Regency architecture. Kemp employed architects Charles Busby and Amon Wilde to create 106 majestic townhouses. Enter Lewes Crescent from its eastern side and you'll see plaques marking notable Victorian residents, including prime minister Lord John Russell. To the north is Sussex Square, with views across the woodland of the enclosures, a private garden with beach access for residents. Following the crescent south, you'll come to Chichester Terrace, where palms sway in front of glass balconies. Heading west along Marine Parade, you'll find the idiosyncratic black-tiled homes on Royal Crescent, where Laurence Olivier lived at no.4 between 1961 and 1979.

Start from Lewes Crescent, BN2

41

DITCHLING BEACON TO DEVIL'S DYKE

An accessible walk in the South Downs

Hazy views of the Sussex Weald make this seven-mile stretch of the South Downs Way special. The fact you can take the 79 bus from town to Ditchling Beacon and hop on the 77 from Devil's Dyke to get back means there's no excuse not to pack your walking boots. Cleaving to the top of the ridge, the path passes a pair of beautiful dew ponds before giving walkers the chance to drop down to the wonderful Jack and Jill Windmills at Clayton. Undulating towards Pyecombe, the route ends up at the top of Devil's Dyke, the largest dry valley in the UK. It's worth waiting until you get back to town for a richly deserved pint at local favourite The Bee's Mouth (no.53).

Start from Ditchling Beacon, BN6 8RJ
nationaltrust.org.uk/visit/sussex/devils-dyke

42

PALACE PIER

The city's most iconic seaside stop-off

When it was completed in 1899, the Palace Pier was the third such attraction to open in Brighton, and it remains an essential stop-off now. With the Chain Pier destroyed by a storm in 1896 and the West Pier finally finished off by fires in 2003, it's your only option for some proper kiss-me-quick seaside action, and it leans into its history hard. There's a riotously loud arcade, tarot readings in a vintage Traveller caravan and surprisingly decent fish and chips available from Palm Court (although beware thieving seagulls), all helping it retain its late Victorian charm. A log flume and rollercoaster bring more modern thrills, but it's better to save your cash for the one-armed bandit machines.

Madeira Drive, BN2 1TW
brightonpier.co.uk

43

BEACH BOX SPA

Saunas on the beach

There's a pleasingly chilled vibe at Beach Box Spa, which is open all year round but comes into its own as the days shorten and the air gets crisp. Set around a fire pit, there are three saunas to choose from: two converted horse boxes with (just enough) space for six, and a stunning 12-person purpose-built cedar sauna with a huge picture window offering views out to sea. On calm days, the English Channel doubles up as a plunge pool, with flip-flops provided to ease passage over the pebbles. When it's windy, a roll-top bath filled with icy water is ideal for cooling off after a sweaty session. Opt for a salt scrub and hair mask to ensure total relaxation.

Banjo Groyne, 285 Madeira Drive, BN2 1EN
beachboxspa.co.uk

44

HOVE BEACH

A low-key alternative to Brighton's main beach

If the section of beach around Shelter Hall at the height of summer feels like the seventh circle of hell, that's because it is. Thousands pour straight down Queen's Road from the train station to the seafront, making Brighton's beach a deeply unrelaxing experience on the hottest days of the year. Far better to stroll west, past the 1360 observation tower and on towards Hove. Here the promenade widens and the beach is broken into sections by groynes. The lack of pubs and clubs makes for a more sedate atmosphere, one where lounging and paddling are the primary concerns. Be sure to get an ice cream from the iconic Marrocco's, just past the end of Hove Lawns.

Hove Beach, BN3 2JJ

45

BOOTH MUSEUM OF NATURAL HISTORY

A Victorian view of the natural world

Founded in 1874 by naturalist, ornithologist and keen hunter Edward Booth on the grounds of his home (the appropriately named Bleak House), the Booth Museum features over 300 cases showing dioramas of British birds in their 'natural' habitats. An avid collector, Booth's dream was to showcase every British species of bird, and filled his study with taxidermied animals. A recreation of this space is the most ghoulish and fascinating of the rooms here, with comfy chairs for spending time flicking through old photo albums or rifling through Booth's own desk, stuffed with shells and trinkets. Today, the Booth collection is supplemented by 525,000 insects, 50,000 minerals and rocks and 30,000 plants.

194 Dyke Road, BN1 5AA
brightonmuseums.org.uk

46

BRIGHTON MUSEUM
AND ART GALLERY

The best place to discover Brighton's history

A minute's walk from the Royal Pavilion (no.48) and housed in the same complex as the Brighton Dome concert hall, the Brighton Museum and Art Gallery does a stellar job of representing the city's past and present. Its permanent collection houses incredible archaeological finds, with Ice Age skeletons and Bronze Age tools discovered locally, right through to images and artefacts highlighting the people who helped create modern Brighton. These include Martha Gunn, an 18th-century swimmer who fostered a culture of women braving the waves, and pioneering suffragette Minnie Turner. The excellent Queer the Pier exhibition uses oral history, film and fashion to show how Brighton became the heart of the UK LGBTQ+ community.

Royal Pavilion Gardens, BN1 1EE
brightonmuseums.org.uk

47

DUKE OF
YORK'S CINEMA

A beautiful, listed movie theatre

The 20-foot pair of can-can dancer's legs on the roof pay testament to the fact that the Duke of York's is not your average cinema. In fact, it's the oldest purpose-built, continually operating one in Britain, having opened in September 1910. Today, it's run by Picturehouse, which has restored what had become a rundown space hosting illegal punk shows back into a Golden Age of Hollywood stunner. There's one screen, with the best seats up on the balcony, handily placed by the bar for those who require mid-movie sustenance. You're as likely to catch a classic Kurosawa flick as you are the latest Marvel offering. There's nowhere better in town for film fanatics to get their fix.

Preston Road, BN1 4NA
picturehouses.com/cinema/duke-of-york-s-picturehouse

48

ROYAL PAVILION

One-time royal outpost turned incredible museum

Unarguably Brighton's most recognisable and opulent building, the Royal Pavilion was built for the Prince Regent, later King George IV, who began taking the sea air here in the 1780s. Its opulent domes, minarets and vast rooms reflect the prince's wild lifestyle, with work commencing in 1787 before the palace was finished in 1815–22 by renowned Regency architect John Nash. The result is spectacular, from the beautifully restored saloon, replete with silk wall panels, to the banquet room, featuring a nine-metre-high chandelier with six silver fire-breathing dragons. Following George IV's death in 1830, the Pavilion was bought by the town, and it was used as a hospital for Indian soldiers during the First World War.

Royal Pavilion & Garden, BN1 1FN
brightonmuseums.org.uk

49

HARBOUR HOTEL

Affordable top-end hotel with a spa below ground

The Harbour Hotel's location, where West Street meets the seafront, is – depending on your viewpoint – either a great spot in the heart of the action or too close to the chaos of Brighton Beach. Yet step through its doors and this wonderful hotel is an oasis of calm. That's not just down to the rooms, which are beach-themed without ever feeling naff; it's also thanks to the superb subterranean spa. Known as HarSPA, guests can access its saunas, hot tubs and pool free of charge as long as they book directly. But the good news is that non-guests can also book in, either for a short break from the crowds above ground or for a longer day of relaxation.

64 King's Road, BN1 1NA
harbourhotels.co.uk/brighton

50

LANSDOWNE HOUSE

Beautiful rooms in a regenerated townhouse

Lansdowne House's owners Natalie and Tom Sargent took two years to restore this Regency townhouse from a tired B&B, full of woodchip and flimsy stud walls, into a glorious hotel packed with original features. The result is sensational, from the richly detailed cast iron balustrades of the main staircase to the cornicing in each of the four bedrooms and the private apartment in the old pantry downstairs. Originally designed by Charles Busby, also responsible for Brunswick Square, the interiors don't lean too heavily on the Georgian style, with sharp mid-century coffee tables and vintage Japanese prints adorning the walls. A luxury stay that will leave some cash available for exploring the superb dining scene on nearby Church Road.

45 Lansdowne Place, BN3 1HF
lansdownehousehove.co.uk

51
ARTIST RESIDENCE

Individually designed rooms by the West Pier

Brighton isn't lacking when it comes to bang average B&Bs charging a small fortune for ugly, cramped spaces. Mercifully, it's also home to smart, carefully thought out hotels like Artist Residence. Set on Regency Square and just a five-minute walk from the quiet expanse of Hove beach, its rooms are designed by different local artists, each one a triumph. These range from tiny, sea view options through to a full on five-star bunkhouse and serviced apartments with roll-top baths. The latter cater perfectly for groups of friends spending a weekend exploring what Brighton has to offer.

33 Regency Square, BN1 2GG
artistresidence.co.uk

52

THE WELL

Amazing Kemptown bar and bottle shop

The Well stands out from all other Brighton watering holes, and not just for its shabby chic aesthetic, which appears to rely on grabbing every upcycled mid-century chair and table from North Laine's second-hand furniture shops. The former off-licence is now a wonderfully convivial space with help-yourself fridges and a small bar serving brews from around the world, as well as the delicious fruity Lonely Palm, made in-house. Out the back, in a former storeroom, is an extra area with views out to sea. While the action spills out on to the street in summer, The Well truly comes alive in winter, when its low light and cosy atmosphere offer a respite from relentless gales and endless rain.

102 St George's Road, BN2 1EA
instagram.com/the_well_brighton

53

THE BEE'S MOUTH

Hove pub with a fun, creative edge

This tiny boozer on Western Road isn't like the old-school pubs you'll find close by, great as they are. Some might call it quirky, thanks to the dismembered mannequins found around the bar, but that does a disservice to what is a proper community hang-out. In summer, the action tumbles out on to the street, with the windows open wide. Yet this dingy space is best enjoyed indoors, from the booths that line the walls to the basement, which hosts the best new local bands, screenings of vintage cinema classics and even drawing and collage classes. The craft beer selection is impressive, while the wine is way better than what you'll find in lesser establishments.

10 Western Road, BN3 1AE
instagram.com/thebeesmouth

54

HAND IN HAND

Homemade ales in a cosy space

Brewing its own beers on site since 1989, the Hand in Hand has grown into a community institution, a corner pub that welcomes all comers into its living room-sized bar. Owner Jen Left is something of a local hero, spotted cycling around Kemptown during lockdown, delivering beers from a model replica of the pub itself. The establishment continues to serve delicious offerings, including its own Toadlicker, a grapefruit-infused pale ale available in cans designed by local artist and pub regular David Shrigley. Pop by on a Sunday for the regular jazz sessions or drop in any time for a game of Toad in the Hole, a Sussex-only pub game that involves tossing coins into a hole on a table.

33 Upper St James's Street, BN2 1JN
handbrewco.com

55

THE GREAT EASTERN

Whiskey, tunes and a classic Brighton welcome

Come Friday night, the only issue with The Great Eastern is finding a seat. Its popularity among ale lovers, whiskey fiends and fans of old-school tunes means you need to arrive early to bag a decent spot. There's a revolving cast of DJs spinning vinyl at the end of the bar, playing vintage country and honky-tonk alongside classic blues, reggae and rocksteady. There's no musical snobbery here, though. The bar staff love a natter and are happy to talk you through the ludicrously extensive spirits list, while the pack of regulars lining the bar ensure there's a resolutely welcoming Brighton vibe. There are a few seats outside, but this place is all about late nights indoors with pals.

103 Trafalgar Street, BN1 4ER
instagram.com/thegreateasternbrighton

56

BLACK DOVE

Killer tunes and great beers

Right at the top of St James's Street, where the party is less full on than in the bars at its western end, The Black Dove has carved out a reputation as one of Brighton's finest pubs. That's down to having over 70 beers available on tap and in the fridge, from your usual big-name craft beers through to niche Belgian Trappist offerings. The wine list is 100 per cent organic too. It's not just about the drinks, though. Music is key here, with DJs spinning foot-stomping R&B 45s, the latest jazz tunes from London courtesy of a monthly night hosted by 22a Records and the Chop Source session, an evening of 1960s and 70s Afrobeat.

74 St James's Street, BN2 1PA
blackdovebrighton.com

57

LEGENDS

Legendary spot at the heart of LGBTQ+ Brighton

The western end of St James's Street and Kemptown is the heart of Brighton's LGBTQ+ scene, regarded for decades as a safe space for true self-expression. And while there is no shortage of great places to party, Legends takes top billing thanks to its always stellar line-up and loving embrace of all dancers. Its terrace looks out to sea, and you can even stay here in its 40-room hotel, but the action centres on the bar and basement club. While weekends offer the chance to go wild until the small hours, there's drag cabaret and comedy every night upstairs: look out for local favourite Davina Sparkle in particular. This is Brighton at its brilliant best.

31–34 Marine Parade, BN2 1TR
legendsresortbrighton.com

58

GREEN DOOR STORE

Indie gig venue open every night

Tucked away beneath the arches of Brighton's Victorian train station, Green Door Store is the prime destination for grassroots music fans and lovers of classic indie nights. The venue can hold 300 on a club night and just 170 when bands are on, making it intimate without ever feeling overcrowded. Local bands take up most of the roster, but expect plenty of breakout acts from across the UK and the States as well. Beloved by the kids and the city's contingent of 6 Music Dads alike, the vibe is friendly and chilled and the beer selection includes Brooklyn Defender, a cut above the weak overpriced lager usually found in rival establishments.

Units 2, 3 & 4, Trafalgar Arches, BN1 4FQ
thegreendoorstore.co.uk

IMAGE CREDITS

CONTRIBUTORS

Joe Minihane is a Brighton-based writer and travel journalist. He is the author of wild swimming memoir *Floating* and his travel writing has appeared in the *Guardian*, *The Sunday Times*, the *Independent* and the *Evening Standard*. When not swimming in the sea near his Kemptown home, he can be found indulging his cappuccino and cinnamon bun habit in Brighton's best coffee spots.

Ellen Richardson is a Brighton-based food and lifestyle photographer working with venues, brands and events across the hospitality industry.

Hoxton Mini Press is a small indie publisher based in east London. We make books about London (and beyond) with a dedication to lovely, sustainable production and brilliant photography. When we started the company, people told us 'print was dead'; we wanted to prove them wrong. Books are no longer about information but objects in their own right: things to collect and own and inspire. We are an environmentally conscious publisher, committed to offsetting our carbon footprint. This book, for instance, is 100 per cent carbon compensated, with offset purchased from Stand for Trees.

INDEX

An Opinionated Guide to Brighton
First edition, first printing

Published in 2023 by Hoxton Mini Press, London
Copyright © Hoxton Mini Press 2023. All rights reserved.

Text by Joe Minihane
Copy-editing by Felicity Maunder
Proofreading by Florence Ward
Additional design by Richard Mason
Production and editorial support by Megan Baffoe

With thanks to Matthew Young for initial series design.

Please note: we recommend checking the websites listed for each
entry before you visit for the latest information on price, opening times
and pre-booking requirements.

A CIP catalogue record for this book is available from the British Library.

ISBN: 978-1-914314-38-4

Printed and bound by OZGraf, Poland

Hoxton Mini Press is an environmentally conscious publisher, committed
to offsetting our carbon footprint. This book is 100 per cent carbon
compensated, with offset purchased from Stand For Trees.

For every book you buy from our website, we plant a tree:
www.hoxtonminipress.com